Anonymous

The Discipline of the Primitive Methodist Church in Canada

Anonymous

The Discipline of the Primitive Methodist Church in Canada

ISBN/EAN: 9783744747561

Printed in Europe, USA, Canada, Australia, Japan

Cover: Foto ©Lupo / pixelio.de

More available books at **www.hansebooks.com**

ADVERTISEMENT.

Eleven years since the Discipline of the Canadian Primitive Methodist Church was published, having been compiled by the Rev. John Davidson. The work was accepted by the Conference; and a large impression was disposed of. During these years the *Body* has made a measure of progress in numbers, Finances, and Church property. Also in this space of time, many new by-laws have been made, and old ones modified, by succeeding Conferences. No copies of the Discipline remain to be sold; while many officials and young ministers have not in their possession the Minutes of Conferences that contain the new rules and modifications, to which reference has been made.

These facts rendered it an absolute necessity to have the Discipline re-compiled, embracing the additions and modifications, for the future guidance of the Church.

We have endeavoured to simplify some parts that appeared ambiguous, and to classify the various rules, on the whole, with as much exactness, as probably, can be expected. It has also been our object to combine *clearness* and *brevity* with a faithful expression of the sense contained in the laws and modifications now consolidated in this Book of Discipline. May it prove useful, in its own sphere, for the enlargement and building up of the Church of Jesus Christ.

On behalf of the Commitee,

THOS. CROMPTON.
WM. BEE.
H. HARRIS.

THE DISCIPLINE

OF THE

Primitive Methodist Church

IN CANADA,

APPROVED BY CONFERENCE.

Let all things be done decently and in order.—1 Cor. 14, 40.

TORONTO:
PUBLISHED BY WILLIAM BEE,
MISSION OFFICE AND BOOK STORE,
107 YONGE ST.
1873.

PREFACE.

THE Primitive Methodist Church is an original Community, not founded in schism, nor in ecclesiastical agitation.

Its first Members were converted from the world; and on the establishment of English Camp Meetings by Hugh Bourne and William Clowes, the REVIVAL, by God's providence, took the form of a distinct Denomination.

This Body in Britain now takes rank amongst Methodist Communities next the Wesleyan in numerical strength, Missionary power, and success in the salvation of sinners.

In 1830 a mission was formed in Toronto, which has been enlarged through a portion of Western Canada.

In 1853 the English Conference made the Canadian stations into a separate Conference, for the purpose of more effectually carrying on the work of God; but the English and Canadian conferences are still united.

The Laws by which the Connexion is governed have been in use from the commencement in Canada; but the Conference of 1860 directed that a BOOK OF DISCIPLINE should be *compiled*, suited to the Church in this country.

That Book of Discipline being now out of print; and alterations and new Rules having been made during the last eleven years, it was found necessary to consolidate these various regulations, and embody them in a new publication of the Discipline.

ALPHABETICAL INDEX.

A

	Page.	Rule.
Applications to erect Churches, &c.	8	34
Allowance to Ministers	13	59-62
" "	51	260

B

Branch Stations Defined	25	138
" Quarterly Meetings	"	139
Book Steward Elected	16	72
Vice " "	28	152
Book Roll	16	56

C

Conference—Constitution of	15	68
" How Organized	"	69-70
" Business Course	"	71-92
Candidates for the Ministry—Written Answers	10	52
" Must give a Pledge	11	54-55
" Examination of	44	230
Credentials of Ministers	32	173
" " Local Preachers	"	174
" " Members	"	176
Conveyance of Church Property	7 / 46	33 / 236
" " Church Property Recorded	8	36
" " " Reported	50	254
" " " Being Sold	8	35
Church Building on Missions	50	255
" Deeds Deposited	37	198

INDEX.

	Page.	Rule.
Complaints—Course to be Adopted	4	15
Circuit Reports for District Meeting	24	132
" Documents Enclosed	25	137
Committee—*Circuit* do., Election and Powers	"	140
" Meetings and Duties	26	141-142
" *Mission*, do., Powers of	"	143
" *Stationing* do., Election of	21	108
" Duties of	18	94-5
" *General*, do., Constitution and Powers	"	97-99
" " Examines and Decides Personal Appeals	19	100
Sanction required for Ministers taken out	10	52
Proceedings laid before Conference	19	103-104
" *Executive*, do—How Composed	29	157
Its Duties	"	158-9
Powers not Possessed	"	160
" *District* do—Constitution	21	113
Duties and Powers	"	114-116
" *Missionary*, do—How Composed	28	153
Duties and Powers	"	154
" *Book*, do—How Elected and Composed	30	161
Duties	"	162
" Preparatory, do—Its Duties	"	163
" Ordination, do—Examines Annual List—Candidates	"	164
" *Central Examination* Do. Constitution	42	223
" " Duties of	"	224-5
" *District Examination* Do. Duties of	43	127-9
" Finance—Do., Elected	21	109
" "	50	252
Church Services—Baptism, Infant	53	
" Adult	57	
Matrimony	60	
Funeral	69	
Lord's Supper	67	
Church Dedication	75	

D

	Page.	Rule.
Doctrines—Primitive Methodist	1	1
Deeds—Form of	7	33
Delegation to District Meeting and Conference	17	87
" "	19	105
" "	21	107
" "	20	106
" "	49	248
Deficiency of Ministers Salary	13-49	59-250
District Meeting—How Composed and Course of Business	19	105-112

E

	Page.	Rule.
Editor's Election—and time of office	16 / 47	72 / 239
Extraordinary Income	50	151

F

	Page.	Rule.
Family Visiting and note	12	56
Furniture and House Rent of Ministers	14	61
Fund—Church and Parsonage	33	184
Terms of Loans	34	186
Applications to	34	187
Connexional Property only has Allowance	35	188
How Sustained	36	190
Officers and Management	"	191
" *Mission*—How Raised and Disposed of	37	199-200
" *Relief*—How Created and its Purpose	38	203
Amount of Allowance	"	205
Time Allowed for	38-9	206-10
Duty of Station respecting this Fund	39	208-9
" *Conference* " How Raised, &c	"	211-12
" *Childrens* " Allowance for Children	40	215-16
Payment of Mission Circuits	51	256

	Page.	Rule.
Fund—*Beneficent* " How Supported	40	217-18
" Allowance to Sup. Ministers	"	219
" " To Widows	41	220
" " To Children	42	221
Collections For	42	222

G

Grants—Annual to Misisons	14	60

H

Horses—Ministers Allowance for	14	62
Hours of Public Service in Church	31	165-6

J

Juvenile Missionary Collections	51	257

L

Leaders—Appointment of	27	149
" Election Annually	7	29
" Duties of	5-6	21-30
" Assistant	27	150
Leader's Meeting—Constitution	26	145-7
" " Court of Appeal	27	148
" " Gen. Duties of	27	151
Local Preachers—Examination &c.	9	46
" " Candidates	10	50
" " Position in the Church	9	47-8
" " Hired	10	49
" " Do. Delegates to Conference	49	249
Legislation	24	133
"	28	54
"	21	116
"	20	105-8

INDEX.

M

	Page.	Rule.
Motions at Official Meetings	3	5
Members—Admission of	4	11-12
" Addendance at Class	4	13
" Complaints—Course of proceeding	4	15
" Contributions	5	19
" Removing	5	18
" Re-admission of official and unofficial	5	20
Ministers—Itinerent, called and employed	10	51-53
" Allowance of	13	59-62
" Probationer's and annual		
" List Minister's Allowance	} 51	260
" Superintendents—Official Duties	12	56-7
" Probationers 1st year of Travelling	47	240
" Course of Study	45	223
" Marrying	47	241
" Journal	48	242
" Smoking	"	243
" University Studies	"	244
" Annual List—Received	16	75
" Superannuated Travelling Expenses	48	245
" Seat and voice in Conference	"	246
" Resignation of	46	233
" Removing	47	238
" Expenses of Removing	14	63
Mission Circuits and Minister's Removing Expenses	49	247
" Allowance of Missionary money	37	201

O

Ordinary Income	14	65-67

P

Preparatory principles at Official Meetings	2	2-10
Presidents' duties	2-3	3-10
" Privilege of voting	2	4
Pledges of Stations and Probationers	11-12	54

Q

	Page.	Rule.
Quarterly Meeting—Constitution of............	22	117
" " Business Course............	"	118-131
" " Branch and Mission Quarterly Meetings..............	25	139
" " . Additional duties of.......	24	132-137

R

Report—Circuit Report....................	24	132
"	20	c
" Standing and other Committee Reports	16	73-82
" Missionary Reports	38	202
Roll Book	4	13
" In Keeping of Ministers	12	56
Reserve List of Ministerial Candidates	19	101
Reading Rules	51	258

S

Steward—Circuit Stewards, duties of..........	8	38-40
" Mission Steward—same powers	9	42-45
" Book Steward—Election of	16	72
Vice " "	28	156
Society Rules—Leader to furnish copy	6	26
Support of Ministers	6-50	25-253
Secretary, General, and Missionary............	28	155-156
" of Conference......................	17	91-2
Singing services controlled by Quarterly Meeting.	31	167
Sabbath Schools—Subject to Quarterly Meeting.	"	168-9
" " Establish Primitive Methodist.	"	170
Stationing, Memorials on.....................	18	94
Study, Course of required.....................	45	223
Schedules, printed...........................	24	132
Sunday Schools—Constitution of	80	

T

	Page.	Rule.
Trustees—Chosen and assigned duties.........	7	31-37
Treasurer General Elected...................	16	72
Temperance—Encourage Temperance Societies..	33	179
" Officials and candidates for office ———requested to abstain..............	33	182-3

DISCIPLINE

OF

The Primitive Methodist Church,

IN CANADA.

DOCTRINES.

1. The Primitive Methodist Body holds the Canonical Books of the OLD AND NEW TESTAMENTS, in the present venerable and authorized version, and believes the following Doctrines as are contained in those Testaments are Fundamental and Evangelical ; and no person can be allowed to hold Office in the Church who is known to promulgate any Doctrines contrary to those herein *briefly* expressed :

Man's innocency in his first state.—Gen. i. 27.—Eccl. vii. 29.

The fall of man, and his consequent depravity.—Gen. iii. 6. Psalm li. 5. Rom. v. 19. Eph. ii. 3.

The general, full, and free redemption of man by Jesus Christ.—Isa. liii. 5. John iii. 16, 17. Heb. ii. 9. 1 John i. 7.

Repentance.—Matt. iii. 8. Mark vi. 12. 2 Cor. vii. 10.

Justification by faith.—Rom. iv. 5. James ii. 18. Rom.

The Witness of the Holy Spirit to our adoption into the family of God.—Rom. viii. 16. Gal. iv. 6.

Sanctification by the Holy Spirit, producing inward and outward holiness.—Ezk. xxxvi. 27. 1 John i. 7. 1 Thess. v. 23.

The doctrine of a Tri-une God.—Deut. vi. 4.—Matt. iii. 16, 17. John x. 30. John xvi. 14, 28.

The Divinity of the Lord Jesus Christ.—John v. 23. Acts v. 31. Heb. i. 8. John viii. 56.

The Resurrection of the Dead, both of the just and the unjust.—John v. 28, 29.—1 Cor. xv. 20.

General Judgment.—Matt. xxv. 31. 2 Cor. v. 10.

Eternal Rewards and Punishments.—Mark x. 30.—Matt. xxv. 46. Mark ix. 44.

PREPARATORY PRINCIPLES

TO BE OBSERVED IN ALL OFFICIAL MEETINGS.

2. Every Official Meeting must open and close with prayer; and when extended beyond an hour, prayer must be offered at suitable intervals.

3. The first business is to elect a President and Secretary. The President's duty is to preserve order; receive propositions, and when discussed, put them to the Meeting; and to declare the decision of the majority.

4. The President, as a Member of the Meeting, has a right to move a resolution, and to vote; and also in case of an equal number of votes, to give a casting vote, in addition to his vote as a member of the assembly.

5. Before an original motion is put, an amendment **may** be submitted, which then takes precedence of the original motion, and must be first put to the meeting; if carried, it supersedes the original motion; but if not, the original is put. Sometimes it will occur, that both the original motion and amendment may be voted out; in that case, a new resolution is submitted, discussed, and put to the meeting for decision. If this course is not adopted, an amendment to the amendment may be submitted. Before any discussion, all motions require to be seconded.

6. An Official meeting, at a subsequent period, may change or rescind any decision to which it may have arrived during its sitting.

7. In the District Meetings and Conference, resolutions proposed must be in *writing*, and handed to the President.

8. No speaker shall address the President on any subject more than *once*, explanations excepted. The President to judge and determine; but movers and seconders have a right to reply.

9. Members of official meetings, who address the President, are strongly desired to speak *briefly*, and to the question, that valuable time may not be wasted.

10. The duty of the Secretary is to record in a book all the resolutions approved by a meeting; and at the close, they shall be read and signed on behalf of the meeting, **by** the President and Secretary.

THE CHURCH,

AND ITS OFFICE BEARERS.

Of Members.

11. Any person who has an earnest desire to flee from the wrath to come may be admitted to meet in class, and received on trial; but it is necessary that the person so received shall give evidence of earnestness in religion three months before being admitted to *full* Membership.

12. No person can be admitted, nor continue in Membership, who attends worldly amusements, frequents taverns, deals in contraband goods or books of immoral tendency, or who is otherwise immoral in conduct.

13. If a member continue absent from the Class, such Member must be visited by the Leader, or some one under his direction. If there be continued neglect for four weeks, and no satisfactory reason assigned, then such Member may be removed from the Circuit Roll Book; but every case must be decided finally by a Leaders' Meeting.

14. A Member wishing to remove to another Class shall inform the Leader or minister; the case must then be submitted to a Leader's Meeting to determine.

15. Should any cause of complaint or offence arise between any of the Members, the course to be pursued must be that laid down in Matthew xviii. 15, 16, 17. "If thy brother shall trespass against thee go and tell him his fault between thee and him alone; if he shall hear thee thou hast gained thy brother. But if he will not hear thee, then take with thee one or two more, that in the mouth of two or three witnesses, every word may be established. And if he shall neglect to hear them, tell it unto the church; but if he neglect to hear the church, let him be unto thee as an heathen

man and a publican." Application must in the second instance be made to the Leader or Minister, and if necessary to the Leaders' Meeting; but no opinion must be given until *both* sides are carefully examined.

16. Any Member removing from one station to another, is desired to apply to the Minister for a credential, that he may be received into the Church at the place where he may locate.

17. All our single Members are admonished not to enter the marriage bond with those whose lives and conversation are not according to the Gospel.

18. All our Members are desired to promote the observance of the Sabbath; the reading of the Holy Scriptures and Family Prayer; to observe Temperance; Visiting the Sick in their affliction; to avoid the company of the wicked; and to shun the appearance of evil.

19. That as our Itinerent Ministers are supported *entirely* by the free-will offerings of the people, it is affectionately desired that each Member subscribe what he can afford, at the Quarterly Renewal of the Tickets. Weekly contributions or offerings are strongly recommended.

20. The Re-admission of Members is the receiving again into Society those who have been separated. The re-admission of unofficial members must be proposed by Leaders' Meetings to Quarterly Meetings; but the re-admission of those formerly *official* requires the further sanction of the District Committee; also, if the party has been an Itinerant Minister, the sanction of the General Committee is also necessary to his re-admission into Society.

Of Leaders.

21. Each leader must make it a point of duty to attend his class as often as possible, and prayerfully study to impart

to his members spiritual and useful instruction, drawn from the word of God and Christian experience. When leading his class he must accustom himself to short speaking, especially when his class is large; and must train his members to be short in speaking and in prayer, that as many as possible may have the opportunity of engaging in those important exercises.

22. It is the duty of a Leader to meet his Class once a week, precisely at the time appointed.

23. The Leader must bring his Class Book, and at the close of the Meeting fill up the blank spaces in relation to "absence," being "present," &c., that his book may be *fit* for presentation at the Leaders' Meeting.

24. The Leader must occasionally employ the Assistant Leader (if any) to assist him; and train his Members to pray at the close, in *quick* succession. The Meeting to continue not longer than *one hour*, extraordinary cases excepted.

25. He is required, at the meeting prior to the renewal of the Tickets, to bring before his people the matter of the Ministers' support; and desire the attendance of *all*, with their contributions, at the Quarterly Visitation and Renewal of the Tickets by the Minister.

26. He must furnish a copy of the Society's Rules to each Member on trial, and labour to train his Members in the polity of the Church; and watch for their souls as one that must give an account to the great Shepherd and Bishop of souls.

27. When a member has been absent from class, either the Leader or his deputy must visit the absentee, to ascertain the cause of his or her absence, and to give suitable advice. Each Leader should form a visiting company in his class, from which to depute persons to visit absentees when neither he nor his assistant leader is able to visit them.

28. Each Leader must sign the list of members of his class inserted in the Rule Book, for the purpose of reporting them to the Quarterly Meeting of the station, and to the District Meeting and Conference. He must not sanction the insertion of the names of persons in the roll book but those who have been received by the Leader's Meeting; nor must he sanction the keeping off the roll book the names of persons who are acknowledged by such meeting.

29. Each Leader shall be subject to annual election at the May Quarterly Meeting. Such nominations may be with the classes, to be confirmed by the Quarterly Meeting. No new class Leaders must be appointed who use intoxicating liquors as a beverage.

30. The Leader must co-operate with the Minister in furnishing the statistics of his class at the *appointed time*, to be inserted in the Schedules at Quarterly Meeting for District Reports to Conference.

Of Trustees.

31. The Trustees of our Churches are nominated by the Quarterly Meetings; and must be Members of Society, or moral and acceptable Members of the Congregations in their respective localities. When they accept their Trust, they are required to hold periodically Trustee Meetings, at which a Minister on the Station *must* be present.

32. They must keep a Book, in which must be recorded all their proceedings and statements of accounts, annually balanced and audited.

33. Trustees under the direction of the Minister, where New Churches are erected, must use the Conveyance Deed prepared under the authority of Conference, which may be had of the Book Steward. A duplicate copy of the deed must

be prepared for recording, and sent to the county registry office.

34. All applications to erect Churches or Parsonages must be laid before the respective Quarterly Meetings, with all requisite information, in order to receive official sanction.

35. Trustees, before they can dispose of Church or Parsonage Property, must have the written authority of Conference.

36. All Church and Parsonage Deeds should be *recorded* within a year; if they are not, they will be *null* and *void:* and New Deeds will have to be executed!

37. Trustees are earnestly desired to see that our Connexional property is insured.

Of Circuit Stewards.

38. A circuit Steward is elected by the Quarterly Meeting, and must be an acceptable and business person. He is the Circuit Treasurer, and attends to the Financial affairs of the Circuit, of which he shall keep an account in a separate book from the Quarter Day book, which must be in the care of the superintendent.

39. In the *full* Quarterly Meeting, the accounts of the Circuit Steward must be read and signed before he be elected, or re-elected, for the next succeeding quarter.

40. He is a Member of all Official Meetings, for Circuit business; and it is his duty to guard against the neglect of preaching appointments on the Station, under the direction of the Superintendent Minister and Circuit Committee.

41. A Mission Steward, on a Mission Station, corresponds with a Circuit Steward on a Circuit, in relation to similar powers and duties of office.

Of Society Stewards.

42. The Society Steward is the Treasurer of the Society's Money where he is located.

43. He is provided with a Book, in which he enters the Society's Quarterly Income, distinguishing the sums raised by each Class; the Quarterly Collections, and other monies received.

44. He provides for the Lovefeasts, Sacraments, and attends to these Ordinances, and sees they and other notices are duly published.

45. He is a Member of the Quarterly and Leaders' Meetings, to which he is amenable.

Of Local Preachers.

46. Local preachers are proposed, at Quarterly Meetings, to labour occasionally in the Ministry: first as Exhorters; afterwards, Preachers on Trial; and full accredited Preachers on the Preachers' Plan. Their doctrinal views must be given in writing, at their examination. No person must be admitted on the plan till he have been examined as to his views on doctrine. The principal doctrinal views of every Candidate must be presented to the Quarterly Meeting in writing subscribed by himself and the Minister present at his examination; and the document shall be preserved by the station for reference.

47. Every Local Preacher must meet in Class; be a lover of discipline and *peace;* and be subject to his Quarterly Meeting.

48. He must be generally acceptable in his ministrations; "apt to teach"; and he is especially recommended to preach *short;* and in his life and conversation to "adorn the gospel of God his Saviour in all things."

49. A Hired Local Preacher is one *hired* for a short period, to supply when needed. He must be unembarrassed in his circumstances when employed; and give a pledge if required peaceably to retire from the work for which he was temporarily hired as a supply.

50. Candidates for the Local preacher's plan shall be asked, "are you a total abstainer from all intoxicating drinks?" The answer must be in the affirmative, if the party be received.—(1862 p. 14.)

Itinerent Ministers.

51. The Itinerant Ministers are called to their office from the Local Preachers, by Circuits, or the General Missionary Committee; and in relation to their *call*, the following regulations are applicable.

52. When the General Committee is applied to, to sanction the taking out of a single Minister, on four years probation, that Committee, by a *special* Committee, must require written answers to the following questions, from

THE CANDIDATE.

a. What are his name and age?
b. His employment?
c. His constitution and general health.
d. Is he in debt? If so, to what amount? and what are his means and prospects of payment? This question applies also to hired local preachers who may be employed for any considerable length of time.
e. *Has he made any matrimonial engagement.

---

* If the Candidate has made an engagement, it will be considered no impediment providing the party wait until the probationary period close.

f. Is his piety undoubted?
g. Does he believe our Doctrines?
h. What are his natural abilities?
i. Has he improved his abilities by reading and study?
j. Has he acquired the principles of the English language?
k. Can he write a good business hand?
l. Has he a knowledge of the duties he will be called to perform?
m. Does he love family visiting; and has he active habits?
n. What success has he had in the salvation of souls?

53. When the General Committee gives its sanction to the application, two pledges must be executed, one by the station pledging, and the other by the brother who is being called into the ministry. This must be done at the May Quarterly Meeting. The case must be laid before the next following District Meeting and Conference.

Pledges.

54. The following are the Pledges which must be sent to District Meeting and Conference and which must be accompanied with an historical account of the Candidate.

The Pledge of the Station.

"The quarterly meeting of the station to the Conference.

"DEAR BRETHREN,—We have taken out, to labour as a travelling preacher,   ; and if he should, during the time of his probation, fail through affliction, or misconduct, or neglect of duty, or inefficiency, or any other cause, to perform successfully and acceptably the work of a travelling preacher, in any station to which he may be appointed, we hereby pledge this station to take him back, and give up a preacher, according to rule, in lieu of him. Also we pledge this Station to receive a married preacher at the expiration of five years from this date, if   to whom this pledge appertains, be received into the Annual List within this period, and if a Conference shall think fit to station for the Circuit such a preacher.

"Signed, by order of the Quarterly Meeting of   station, on this   day of May, 18   President.
                                                                                    Secretary."

The pledge of the Candidate.

"To the Conference.

"DEAR BRETHREN,—Having been taken out to labour as a traveling preacher by   Station, and pledged thereby, I hereby solemnly and sacredly promise that I will cultivate and promote peace, soul-saving, and the general good of the Connexion to which I belong, as well as the spiritual good of the brethren, and the stations with which I may be immediately connected; that I will study and practice the Rules of the Connexion, and devoutly discharge those ministerial duties therein prescribed for me, or which may be recommended to me, or enjoined upon me by those meetings or persons to whom I may be Connexionally amenable; and if I fail before the completion of my probation to fulfil these engagements, or otherwise misconduct myself, or if I be not generally received in any station to which I may be sent, or be officially desired to withdraw from the Ministry, I hereby promise that I will withdraw without speaking evil of any party or person in the Connexion, or sowing any discord, or exciting towards myself any sympathy, or countenancing in behalf of myself any petitions; and that I will, at my own expense, either return peacefully to the circuit that took me out and pledged me, or to some other place where I may choose to reside, and that I will there and elsewhere observe the same peaceful conduct as I have herein promised to observe.

"Witness my hand this   day of May, in the year of our Lord one thousand eight hundred and

55. If the Candidate is married, the same pledges must be taken and questions answered (except the fifth), with an account of his children (if any); and the General Committee must forward the whole case to the Conference, which assembly *alone* has the power to take out married preachers.

56. The Superintendent Minister of the Circuit or Mission to which he is appointed by Conference must, on entering on his Station, *immediately* make himself acquainted with all the spiritual and financial matters of his sacred charge, especially the state of the *separate* Societies, by re-entering them in the Roll Book; each Society its *entire* position; the course of service pursued; the holding of Committee and Leaders' Meetings; the state of the Sabbath School; arrang-

ing for the Quarterly Visitation of the Classes; the course of Family Visiting.*

57. Also, it will be necessary for him to make arrangements and attend to the special duties of preparing statistics for the Quarterly Meeting *prior* to Conference; and those duties which *follow after*, on behalf of the whole interests of his Station; and if he has a Colleague, to see that he possesses equal official information; that at the different Official Meetings the Minister or Ministers may be prepared to submit every matter to the Boards, that require consideration and settlement. Also, on leaving a Station, all necessary information must be left for their successors.

58. As the Itinerant Ministers are wholly supported by the Church, to the duties of their *calling* they must give all their energies; and form no connexion with Secret Societies, (Temperance Societies excepted) Political Parties; nor trade, except in Connexional publications, which are designed, by enlightning the people, to forward the great objects of their Holy Ministry.

Allowances of Itinerant Ministers.

59. The salaries of our Ministers shall be, for Towns and Cities $650; for Country Circuits $550; and for back Mission Stations $450, with fuel. In all cases wherein the funds are sufficient to pay the Superintendent Minister to the amount of $450, the young men shall be paid their salary in full. If their be a deficiency in the payment of the last named sum the Station must proportion the deficiency so that the married minister shall sustain two-thirds and the single minister one-third of such deficiency.

---

* A "General Family Visitor" is one who visits on an average, fifteen separate families weekly, throughout the Connectional year; each visit includes giving Religious Instruction, and praying with the households respectively.

60. All Missionaries, on Mission Stations, have Annual Grants, arranged annually by Conference; and the respective Mission Stations are expected to raise the balance *deficient*, to equal the above scale of allowances. Special engagements with the Missionary Committee excepted.

61. Each of our Ministers shall be allowed, by the Station to which he is appointed, a Parsonage, and furnished with articles of *heavy* furniture, including heavy crockery.

62. Also, all Ministers who keep horses, which are not provided for by the Stations, either in whole or in part, shall be allowed $10 per quarter for the same.

63. The removal expenses of Ministers shall be paid by the Quarterly Meetings of the receiving Circuits; and those removing to Mission Stations by the Missionary Committee.

64. Cases of the Superannuation of Itinerant Ministers must be decided by the Conference.

The Ordinary Income of Stations.

65. The first Quarterly Meeting on each Station, after Conference, shall make the needful regulations to raise the amounts for the Minister's Salary, and when they think it expedient, they shall form a Committee, to solicit from the regular hearers quarterly contributions on behalf of the cause of God.

66. "On each Mission Station, our Missionaries, at the quarterly renewal of tickets, shall take the class-book of the Society, and calling the name of each Member, shall kindly ask—what amount shall be put down by him on the class-book as his quarterly thank-offering to the Lord? And that the said quarterage shall be collected by the Leader of the Class."

67. On each Mission Station, the Minister, at the time

of the quarterly renewal of Tickets, shall make it known in each Society that we think it desirable that those members who are unable to pay their Quarterages in money, do as much as possible towards supporting the Mission by contributions of produce; and that all such contributions shall be placed to the account of such members as Quarterage. And that the Steward of each Society shall be expected to collect the said contributions as soon as possible."

Conference.

68. The Annual Conference, which is the highest Court of the Body, whose decisions are final, and without appeal, is constituted of one-third Ministers in full Connexion, and two-thirds Official Laymen, who have been appointed Members in the Church for the past two years; also the General Officers of the Body chosen by the preceding Conference; as the General Committee Delegate, Agent of Friendly Society, General Treasurer, General Missionary Secretary, Book Steward, Editor, and the President and Secretary of the preceding Conference the Secretary being the General-Committee Delegate.

69. Its course of proceedure is for the Ex-President and Secretary to organize the Meeting; to examine the Credentials of the delegates, and decide who shall be admitted as hearers.

70. The Conference being formed, the officers are elected as follows. The President, Secretary, Vice-President; Assistant Secretaries; Letter Writer, Reporters; Messengers; Time Keeper and any other *necessary officer*, and also the hours of session decided.

71. It shall elect the following Committees, viz. Ordination, Temperance, Sabbath observance, and Sabbath schools, and other necessary Committees, to facilitate the labours of the Conference.

72. The following Connexional officers shall be elected (*a.*) The Editor. (*b.*) The Book Steward, and General Missionary Secretary. (*c.*) The General Treasurer.

73. Changes in relation to stations. (*a.*) Division of Stations. (*b.*) Uniting Stations. (*c.*) Missions becoming Circuits, and other changes. (*d.*) New Stations. (*e.*) Additional Preachers wanted. (*f.*) Re-stationing, special cases.

74. Reports of Committees. (*a.*) Central Board of Examiners. (*b.*) District Boards of examiners. (*c.*) Ordination Committee.

75. It shall decide upon the following matters in relation to the ministry. (*a.*) Admission to the annual List. (*b.*) Whose pledges shall be received. (*c.*) What Candidates shall be admitted. (*d.*) Who shall be received on the Reserve List. (*e.*) Resignations. (*f.*) Applications to attend school or College. (*g.*) Any other matters which may need attention.

76. Necessary instructions shall be given to the Granting Committee.

77. It must examine and decide upon all matters of Legislation brought up from the lower Courts.

78. It must examine and decide on all claims on the Relief Fund.

79. Station Reports, relating to matters which have been confirmed by District Meetings.

80. Exceptions to Station Reports. (*a.*) Decreases. (*b.*) Those relating to ministers. (*c.*) Those relating to officials personally. (*d.*) Those relating to the station.

81. Reports of Standing Committees. (*a.*) General Committee. (*b.*) General Missionary Committee. (*c.*) Book Committee. (*d.*) Christian Journal. (*e.*) District Committees.

82. Reports of Conference Committees. (*a.*) Financial

and Statistical. (*b.*) Sabbath Observance and Sabbath Schools. (*c.*) Temperance. (*d.*) Special Committees appointed by the previous Conference. (*e.*) Any other Committees appointed by Conference.

83. It shall examine and decide on all cases relating to Church Property. (*a.*) Churches. (*b.*) Parsonages. (*c.*) Other property.

84. It shall examine and decide all cases of complaints and appeals.

85. It shall appoint a day of Thanksgiving, or Prayer and fasting, and make all necessary arrangements for the Connexion.

86. It shall elect the following officers. (*a.*) General Committee Delegate. (*b.*) Friendly Society Representatives. (*c.*) General Committee Delegates to the following District Meetings. (*d.*) Delegation to the English Conference. (*e.*) Auditors for the ensuing year.

87. It shall decide on the necessary Delegation to the next District Meetings and Conference.

88. It shall appoint the following Committees. (*a.*) General and General Missionary Committees. (*b.*) Executive Committee. (*c.*) Book Committee. (*d.*) District Committees. (*e.*) Central Board of Examiners. (*f.*) District Boards of Examiners.

89. It shall appoint the time and place of holding the next District Meetings and Conference.

90. It shall pass the necessary votes of thanks.

91. The President and Secretary shall be held accountable to next Conference for all the business being done in due order, that there be no irregularities or omissions.

92. It shall read the minutes and direct which shall be published. And the President and Secretary must sign the Conference Journal.

Stationing.

93. Memorials on Stationing must be sent from the May Quarterly Meetings, attached to the Annual Report Forms, on separate sheets, and be properly signed by the chairman and secretary. They must be forwarded from each District Meeting to the Stationing Committee.

94. The limit of a Minister being stationed on a Circuit or Mission shall be THREE years, and the limit of a Probationary Preacher shall be *one* year of the *first* two of his Ministry. But the Stationing Committee and Conference may make an exception for a fourth year's station, in case of a special work of grace that may be in progress on a Circuit or Mission, or if the Stationing Committee finds special difficulty in supplying the Stations, providing such Station applies for its preacher a fourth year.

95. The Stationing Committee, elected by the District Meetings, shall meet the day previous to the Meeting of Conference, and prepare a Draft of the stations, which shall be read the first time in the afternoon of the second day of the Conference sittings. The Draft shall be read a second time before noon on the third day of the Conference, and the third reading, for final revision and confirmation by the Conference, shall take place on the morning of the fourth day of its sittings.

96. When an investigation is entered into by Conference, respecting the moral character of any of its ministers, all hearers shall be requested to withdraw during such investigations.

General Committee.

97. This Committee is elected by the Conference to attend to the General affairs of the Connexion till the following

Conference. It meets quarterly under the direction of Conference, to which court it is responsible.

98. It has between Conferences, the entire government of the Church, being the highest court of appeal and advice.

99. Its Members are composed of Ministers and Official Laymen, including the General Treasurer of the Connexional Funds, the General Secretary, and the same persons as the General Missionary Committee.

100. It receives and examines applications relating to charges and appeals from all parts of the Connexion; and after obtaining all the evidence and facts, it decides accordingly. If it cannot satisfactorily decide, it prepares the cases for the consideration of Conference, through its Secretary.

101. It must keep a reserve list of young men who have been recommended for the ministry by the Quarterly Meetings, and by the Examining Committee to which they have been amenable.

102. It must give advice according to circumstances, to any official meetings and official members, and prudently remonstrate against any infringement by one person or party on the rights of others, and on the laws, usages, and institutions of the Connexion. But no application for advice must be received except it contains all the facts of the case to which it relates.

103. It meets quarterly, at the same time and place as the General Missionary Committee.

104. A yearly Report of all the proceedings of this Committee must be prepared, by its Secretary, and laid before the Conference.

District Meeting.

105. A District Meeting is composed of a General Committee Delegate and those persons whom the Circuits and

Missions, &c., have sent as their Delegates, by appointment of the Conference preceding. A Circuit sends one minister and two laymen ; and a Branch or Mission sends one minister and one layman.

The business course of proceeding is to :—

(*a.*) Receive the Credentials of Delegates.

(*b.*) Receive the Contributions to the different Church Funds ; the General Committee Delegate being the Treasurer (*pro tem.*) on behalf of General Treasurer.

(*c.*) Examine the Reports of Stations, and other Reports, in order ; making Special Minutes of Decreases, &c. Documentary evidence only shall be received in reference to exceptions taken to the Annual Reports of stations.

(*d.*) Examine Applications for the Relief Fund.

(*e.*) Examine all Complaints and Appeals.

(*f.*) Examine New Legislation; and prepare for Conference what may be necessary.

(*g.*) Examine the state of Church Property. Churches, Parsonages and other property.

(*h.*) Examine all *cases* in relation to Candidates for the Ministry, sent by Circuits or General Missionary Committee ; endorse the Pledges, &c.

(*i.*) Receive the Reports of Board of Examiners ; District Committee Report, decide on Preachers' Probations ; and those for the Annual List, &c.

106. It must next elect delegates to the next Conference. *Five* Ministers and *ten* laymen shall be sent from Toronto and *four* ministers and *eight* laymen from Brampton and London Districts ; *three* ministers and *six* laymen from Hamilton and Guelph Districts ; and *two* ministers and *four* laymen from Kingston and Barrie Districts.

107. In electing ministerial Delegates to Conference they shall be chosen from those who are superintendents; and two of them from those who have been elected before, in the Districts that send four or five ministerial delegates, and one who has been before to Conference in the Districts that send two ministers.

108. Elect the Members to compose the Stationing Committee who shall be the General Committee Delegates; two Lay Delegates each from Toronto and Brampton Districts, and one from each of the other Districts. Also elect the respective Vices.

109. Elect the Finance Committee, one minister and two Laymen, each from Toronto and Brampton District, and one Minister and one Layman from each of the other Districts.

110. Appoint the place of next District Meeting.

111. Bind up the District Reports, and place them, and all documents, in the care of General Committee Delegate.

112. Appoint all other needful measures, and Read, and sign the Minutes.

District Committee.

113. This Committee is elected by the District Meeting, and confirmed by Conference. It is composed of Itinerant Ministers and Official Laymen; and may elect one of its Members to represent it in the District Meeting.

114. It acts as Assistant to the General Committee within its District, and is guided by the *same* rules and principles.

115. It gives advice to any Circuit applying; examines complaints and appeals; considers cases of re-admissions; and yields all possible help to the General Committee within its District. It must sanction the building of Connexional

churches and parsonages, and for such purpose must have a proper statement of building cases laid before it.

116. It may Legislate; forward its Legislation to the District Meeting; and must present a yearly summary of its business, duly signed.

Quarterly Meeting.

117. The Quarterly Meeting is composed of Preachers, Stewards, and Leaders; Members of Circuit Committee, with Superintendents of Sabbath Schools, (being Members of the Society,) and is the highest court of a Circuit, Branch, or Mission.

118. It is in the order of time, preceded by holding the Preachers' Meeting, which is formed of Preachers and the Circuit Steward *only*. Its course of proceeding is, to examine all Preachers and Exhorters whose names are on the Plan, in relation to Character, Doctrine, and fulfilling Preaching engagements. All its decisions must be confirmed by the Quarterly Meeting.

119. Its course of business is for the President to call the names of the Local Preachers and inquire if there be any complaint in relation to character, doctrine, acceptability, attention to appointments, &c. If no remark be made, he proceeds to the close of the List; but if any objection be intimated, he marks the case. A similar course is taken with the Itinerant Ministers. Then the next proceeding is, to *examine* the marked cases in rotation.

120. Next business is, to raise Local Preachers on trial to full Preachers.

121. To receive fresh Preachers from abroad, duly credentialed; and Exhorters to be raised to Preachers on Trial; and fresh Candidates to be received as Exhorters.

Quarterly Meeting—Full Board.

122. Its course of business is to read the Places on the Plan; confirm, or vary, as required; and fresh Places taken on.

123. The Ministers and Stewards must submit to the Board their Numerical and Financial Accounts.

124. All charges and allowances of Ministers paid; accounts balanced and signed.

125. No debts to be incurred; nor trenching upon the anticipated funds of the coming quarter.

126. The first Quarterly Meeting of each Station after Conference, shall make the needful regulations to raise the amounts of the minister's salary, and where it is expedient, for a Committee to solicit from the regular hearers quarterly contributions on behalf of the cause of God.

127. If any balance is in the Steward's hands, the Meeting to direct its disposal.

128. The Quarterly Meeting must determine all cases of Complaints or appeals.

129. It must Examine the past Quarter's proceedings of the Circuit Committee; and all other Committees which may have been appointed by the preceeding Quarterly Meeting.

- (*a.*) Station Ministers on Branches if any.
- (*b.*) Examine the position of the Sabbath Schools.
- (*c.*) Appoint Sacraments and Lovefeasts.
- (*d.*) Appoint all open-air Services.
- (*e.*) Elect Circuit and Society Stewards.
- (*f.*) Elect Circuit and Planning Committees.
- (*g.*) Appoint the time and place of next quarterly Meeting.

(*h.*) The February Quarterly Meeting must ascertain if it has any young men qualified to labor as Itinerant Ministers, and if so, must recommend them to the District Board of Examiners, and send such recommendation, with the names of the young men to the secretary of said Board, immediately after the Quarterly Meeting, and also recommend them in the usual way to the following District Meeting and Conference.

130. Any difficult case, must be arranged for the next higher Court.

131. Make all needful Appointments, and read and sign the Minutes.

Additional Duties of the Quarterly Meeting before District Meeting and Conference.

132. To fully prepare the Circuit Report for the District Meeting, in all its *varied particulars*, according to the printed Schedule *authorized* by the Conference.

133. Prepare all legislation which the Meeting wishes the Conference to adopt, with reasons for its adoption.

134. To send, through the District Meeting, to be forwarded to the Stationing Committee, a Memorial of which Preacher or Preachers the Station desires to be appointed to it the ensuing year.

135. All other appointments and arrangements which may be necessary in relation to District Meeting and Conference.

136. The forms of application of Ministers for admission into the Preacher's Friendly Society must be prepared and sanctioned by this Quarterly Meeting, and also Annual List

Forms must be obtained from the Book Steward by probation Ministers ending their probation, which must be properly filled up, and have the sanction of the May Quarterly Meeting. If this is omitted, another year's probation must be served.

137. All documents in connexion with Circuit Reports must be uniform in size, and neatly stitched together.

Branches.

138. A Branch is a part of a circuit which has a distinct preacher's plan and quarterly accounts, a Committee and Steward, preparatory Quarterly Meeting, and other official meetings similar to those of a circuit.

139. Branch and Local Mission Quarterly Meetings exercise similar powers and duties, within their respective Stations, as Quarterly Meetings of Circuits, subject to approval by the parent Circuit and General Missionary Committee's Quarterly Meetings. And it must be distinctly understood that the Quarterly Income of a Branch and of the parent Quarterly Meeting must be devoted to pay the expenses of the whole Circuit.

Circuit Committee.

140. This Committee is elected by the Quarterly Meeting, and is composed of Itinerant Ministers, Circuit Stewards, and of not less than four other *official* or *un-official* Members. This Committee is the Executive of the Quarterly Meeting, and in the intervals of those Meetings carries out all its directions; and all the Officers of the Circuit are amenable to it in such intervals; but in such intervals it cannot dispose of any monies or property belonging to the Station, nor call a Minister out to travel.

141. The Meetings of this Committee are usually held monthly ; and its *special* meetings, in relation to the particular mode of summoning the Members, is laid down by the Quarterly Meeting, at its election.

142. In addition to the regular business of this Committee, the following, among other questions, may be considered necessary to adopt, to revive and carry on the work of God in the Circuit or Station :

- (*a.*) Can our congregation be improved ?
- (*b.*) What is the state of the Classes ?
- (*c.*) Are there any cases of complaints to be adjusted ?
- (*d.*) Has each Class a Leader and Assistant Leader ? and are the Leader's Meetings properly attended ?
- (*e.*) Are the Prayer Meetings properly attended ?
- (*f.*) Are the Quarterages of the Classes duly collected, and paid over to the Steward ?
- (*g.*) Do the Sabbath Schools prosper ?
- (*h.*) Are the Preaching Appointments properly attended to ?

143. A Mission Station has its Mission Committee, which exercises powers and duties similar to a Circuit Committee, on behalf of a Circuit.

144. If any difficult case occur, the Circuit Committee may lay it before the General Committee, with all its necessary facts and circumstances.

Leaders' Meeting.

145. A Leaders' Meeting is composed of the Ministers, Leaders, and Assistant Leaders (who only have voice and vote in the absence of their principal) and Society Steward. When a Leader is unavoidably prevented from attending the

Leader's Meeting, his assistant shall attend as his representative.

146. To constitute a Leaders' Meeting legal, there must be present a Minister; extraordinary cases excepted, of which the Circuit Committee must judge.

147. Where there is only one Class, the Minister and Leader transact the business.

148. The Leaders' Meeting is a Court of Appeal from the decision of Leaders on any misunderstanding, complaint or offence between Members; and usually its meetings are held monthly.

149. Every Leader must attend the Leaders' Meetings; three times absence, without *sufficient reason*, must decide his removal from office; and if found inefficient, or disqualified, his removal must take place. When a new Leader is appointed in the place of one who is not acceptable or has removed, the Class recommends a Leader, if necessary; but the appointment must be confirmed by the Leaders' Meeting.

150. It is the duty of the Leaders' Meeting to appoint Assistant Leaders, who are recommended to lead the Class once a month, under the direction of the Leader.

151. It is the duty of the Leaders' Meeting—

(*a.*) To examine the Class Books.

(*b.*) To make arrangements quarterly for renewing Tickets.

(*c.*) To prepare accounts for Quarterly Meeting at the proper time.

(*d.*) To inquire into and decide on all matters relating to each Class; and the general interests of the Society.

152. If any difficult case occur, which cannot be satisfactorily decided, it must be sent to the Court next higher for examination and settlement.

Missionary Committee.

153. This Committee is elected by the Conference; and its powers embrace the General Management of the Missionary operations of the Church, in the intervals of the Conference.

154. It is composed of the same Members as the General Committee, meets quarterly, at the same time and place; examines the Reports and Journals of Missionaries. It pays Salaries; administers Instructions, Reproofs, Directions to Missionaries; and its efforts are constantly directed to the most effectual ways of working the Missionary System, under the authority of Conference. It has limited powers in calling out Missionaries, and opening fresh Missions; and it has also Legislative Powers, which it may exercise.

Missionary Secretary.

155. The Missionary Secretary, appointed by Conference must carry out all the directions of Missionary affairs in relation to the General Missionary Committee; and must prepare an annual report of all its proceedings, compiled from its Quarterly minutes to be laid before Conference for approval.

Book Steward and General Secretary.

156. Immediately after the election of a Book Steward and Missionary Secretary, the Conference shall elect a Vice to this office. The brother so appointed shall be a member

of the Book Committee, and shall be informed when any important meeting of this Committee is about to be held. . He shall also be present and take part in the annual stock taking ; shall assist in auditing the accounts ; and shall have afforded him, by the principal officer, every reasonable facility for becoming acquainted with the duties of the office.

Executive Committee.

157. This Committee is elected by the Conference, and is composed of the President and Secretary of Conference, with at least six other official persons, including a Corresponding Secretary.

158. It is the Executive of *both* the General and Missionary Committees ; and acts in the intervals of the Quarterly Meetings of the above Committees. Its Meetings are Monthly if necessary ; it receives all Correspondence, and carries out all the measures of the *two* Committees in question ; and has an Official Secretary especially appointed by Conference.

159. If the business of the General and Missionary Committees requires immediate attention, the Executive disposes of it, where delay would be injurious ; but in case of matters of importance, where delay until the regular Meetings of the above Committees would not be injurious, the Executive must arrange the business, and submit it to the Quarterly Meetings.

160. It does not exercise the power of calling out Ministers, nor voting Connexional Funds for any purposes ; but acts simply as an Executive, in carrying out the directions and business matters as aforesaid, through its Secretary, who

must at each quarterly Meeting of the above Committees submit the Minutes of its proceedings for inquiry and approval.

Book Committee.

161. This Committee is elected by the Conference, and is usually composed of the same persons as the Executive Committee, and meets at the same time and place as the Executive.

162. It directs all that relates to the Book Establishment of the Church; and its sanction must be given to all our Church Publications, before publishing; and it must annually, through its Secretary, lay before the Conference a report of its proceedings, compiled from the Minutes of its Meetings during the year.

Preparatory Committee.

163. This Committee is composed of the President and Secretary, with the General Committee Delegates elected by the Conference. It meets on one of the days of the same week in which Conference commences its sittings, to arrange the documents, and draw up the Order of Business, to accellerate the labours of the Conference Assembly.

Ordination Committee.

164. Each Conference shall from its members appoint a Committee composed of one minister from each District, who shall subject to General Examination all probationers recommended for ordination by their respective District Meetings, and shall report at an early stage of the Conference. This Committee to form one of the standing Committees.

Church Hours, &c.

165. It is earnestly desired, that in harmony with Primitive Methodism, all our Religious Services be conducted in a brief and lively manner.

166. The standard of time to be,—On Sabbath Mornings and Afternoons, the entire service not to exceed one hour and a quarter; Evening, one hour and a half; Week Evenings, one hour and a quarter. Special Services and Camp Meetings are excepted.

167. The regulation and control of the Devotional Services, and Singing Services, are in the Quarterly Meetings of the respective Stations in the Body.

Sabbath Schools.

168. All Sabbath Schools within a Station are subject to the direction of the Quarterly Meeting of the Station.

169. Every Itinerant Minister is a Member of *every* School Committee or Teachers' Meeting; and must have access to all Minute Books and *Accounts ;* and all such Books and Accounts may be required by the Quarterly Meeting, for Examination.

170. It is desired that all our Ministers and Official Members make every effort to establish " Primitive Methodist Sabbath Schools," and for them to use the Rules and Hymn Books of the Body in their Management and Devotional Exercises.

171. At each Connexional place of Worship all our Ministers are expected to preach at least once a quarter on the subject of Sabbath Schools, and see that the Reports of

Sabbath Schools are regularly entered in the minute book of each station. (1865, p. 6.)

172. One session of Conference may be devoted to the interchange of views on the subject of Sabbath Schools and Sabbath School work ; and one of the Conference religious services shall be devoted to Sabbath School interests.

Credentials and Certificates.

173. On a Minister removing from one Station to another, he is required to furnish a Credential from the Station he leaves, to that to which he is appointed : such Credential to be received by the Circuit Committee, or Mission Committee, as the case may be.

174. The same course to be observed in relation to a Local Preacher removing.

175. Members, on removing, are desired to apply to the Superintendent Minister, or an Official Meeting, for a Credential, in order to their being received officially in the Station to which they may remove.

176. It shall be the duty of every minister in charge of a station from which a member is removing, to give such member a Credential, and at the same time forward a duplicate copy to the minister of the station in which the removing party is about to locate.

177. Special care is required to be exercised in receiving Credentials from persons from abroad ; if in any case doubt exists, in relation to official individuals, the Superintendent of the Station must write for information prior to receiving such in an official capacity !

178. All Ordained Ministers shall receive the necessary

Temperance.

179. It is earnestly recommended that all our Ministers and Members abstain from using Intoxicating Liquors, as a *beverage;* and to use every prudent effort to encourage Temperance Societies.

180. It is also desired that all our Ministers abstain from the injurious habit of tobacco smoking! and discourage the practice among our members by precept and *example.*

181. In the historical account of Stations to District Meeting and Conference, it shall be asked how many officials are on the station? and how many of them are total abstainers from intoxicating drinks?

182. All Candidates for office in our Church shall be requested to become total abstainers from intoxicating drinks; and all Candidates for Church Membership shall also be requested to do the same.

183. It is strongly recommended that Temperance Societies be formed in our churches, and that every effort be made to influence our people in favor of inducing all members to abstain from intoxicating liquors; and a public temperance meeting be held, or temperance sermon preached at all our appointments.

Church and Parsonage, Loan and Grant Fund.

184. This Fund is established to assist Trustees (where most needed) to purchase suitable sites, and erect Churches and Parsonages, and such other property as may promote the interests of the Connexion.

185. In very needy cases the Committee of management may make Grants to Trustees to aid them in the erection of Churches and Parsonages.

186. The Committee shall make Loans to Trustees applying for aid, on the following terms:—

(*a*.) For every one hundred dollars loaned they shall pay back to the Fund one hundred and ten dollars.

(*b*.) Loans shall be paid back in ten annual instalments, or in less time if the Trustees are able to do it. The terms of payment in this case to be arranged between the Committee and the Trustees.

(*c*.) Trustees who have had the advantage of a Loan, shall, when the debt is paid, donate to the Fund not less than one per cent per annum of the amount of the loan, to aid other needy Churches.

187. All applications for aid from this Fund shall be made in accordance with blank forms to be furnished by the Committee through its secretary, and shall state:—

(*a*.) The number of Church members, Sunday school children, and congregation to be accommodated. The population of the place, and its future prospects.

(*b*.) The location, size, present and prospective value of the site.

(*c*.) A description of the building. But if not yet built, and it is required by the Committee, a copy of the plans and specifications shall be submitted, and if deemed necessary altered according to suggestions.

(*d*.) The estimated cost, when completed. The amount the congregation agrees to raise by subscriptions, collections and other means, what debt will remain, and how soon the congregation will be able to remove it. To what amount the building is, or will be insured; and anything that may aid the Committee in coming to a proper decision.

188. Only Connexional Property shall be entitled to grants or loans. The Deed must be registered. The property must be insured to the amount of three-fourths of its value, and any other liabilities against it must be such as the Committee approves of.

189. The fund shall be sustained as follows :—

(a.) In the month of February a collection shall be taken up annually, at each preaching appointment on each station.

(b.) Subscriptions shall be taken up throughout our work. A subscription of one dollar shall constitute a member for one year. Twenty dollars shall constitute a member for life. Any person who subscribes one hundred dollars to this Fund, or any minister who shall collect that sum, shall be a member of the Committee for life, having a seat and a voice in each meeting. But any person who shall contribute three hundred dollars, or any minister who shall collect that amount, shall be a life member of the Committee, with voice and vote in its meetings for business.

(c.) A subscription of one thousand dollars shall constitute a separate Loan Fund which shall bear the name of the subscriber, or any other name he may designate. This Fund shall be used only as a Loan in aid of Church extention, under the direction of the Committee, and a distinct report of its investment shall be made in the report of the General Fund.

(*d.*) Trustees of Churches, Sabbath schools, Ladies' aids, or other societies contributing ten dollars to the fund shall have honorable mention in the Report. Legacies and Bequests of fifty dollars and upward shall also have the same.

190. The officers of the Fund shall be the following :—President, Vice-President, Secretary and Assistant, and Treasurer, who shall perform the duties usually devolving upon such officers. All officers shall be appointed by the Conference.

191. The management of the Fund shall be in the hands of the officers and a Committee consisting of a minister and a layman for each District, chosen by the District Meetings, subject to the confirmation of Conference. Five members of the Committee present at a meeting, shall constitute a quorum for the transaction of business. The Committee shall meet quarterly the day previous to the General Committee, and the Secretary shall be the convener.

192. Special Meetings may be called by the President, or the Secretary, or any three members of the Committee.

193. The Committee shall carry out the arrangements of Conference, and make necessary suggestions to Quarterly Meetings, in relation to subscriptions, collections, &c., for the Fund, and annually report its doings to the Conference.

194. District Committees shall co-operate with this Committee, and aid it in every possible way in its work of benevolence.

195. It is strongly recommended by the Conference that much prudence be exercised in erecting Churches and Parsonages, that cases of distress may be avoided.

196. In all building cases, leave must be given by a Quarterly Meeting, and District Committee ; such meetings being furnished with all necessary information before giving their approval.

197. It is required, that all our Superintendents see that the connexional form of conveyance be used ; and that all church property be duly registered in the church book kept for that purpose.

198. It is also strongly required that each Superintendent or Circuit Steward on a station have in his *charge* and *custody* all church deeds and other important documents ; enter a notice of them in the quarterly minute book of the Circuit or Mission, and *faithfully* give them to their successors in office.

Missionary Fund.

199. This Fund is created by subscriptions, collections, donations, and grants made in Canada and from England, and is under the control of Conference, and the General Missionary Committee between Conferences.

200. It is *exclusively* devoted to Missionary purposes in Canada ; and all allowances are paid to Missionaries quarterly, on the reception of their Reports by the Missionary Committee ; which committee *alone* has power to dispose of the funds for their lawful purposes, in carrying on the work of God on old and *new* missions.

201. As it is ever *desirable* for old Stations to become self-sutaining, in order to apply the Funds to fresh openings, therefore it is ruled, that to induce this speedily to be done, the *young* Circuit shall retain of its own missionary money in the following ratio :—The first year *three-fourths*, second

year *two-thirds*, third year *one-half*, fourth year, *one-third*, after which it shall be self-sustaining.

Missionary Reports.

202. The annual Missionary Reports, for all the Stations must be made up by the May Quarterly Meetings, and sent immediately, with the Missionary money, to the General Missionary Secretary; and it must be certified on the Annual Report whether such has been done or not.

Relief Fund.

203. This Fund is raised by each Circuit and Mission Station, contributing annually the sum of five cents, per each full Member; and the amount must be entered in the District Minutes. The sum to be taken *in cash* by the Delegate to the District Meeting, to be paid to the General Committee Delegate, that he may pay the total received to the General Secretary, for the General Treasurer prior to Conference. This fund is designed to render assistance to Stations when Ministers are unable through sickness to perform their duty, that needful agency may be provided in the place of sick ministers.

204. If the Minister shall have been sick two weeks, the Station shall apply to the District Meeting and Conference with a full statement of the case, officially signed, and if approved, payment will be made.

205. The allowance from this Fund to a Station shall be—

On account of a Married Minister, $4 00 per week.

On account of a Single Minister, $2 00 per week.

206. There shall be no allowance granted in any case for the first two weeks of sickness.

207 There shall be no allowance made on behalf of any preacher's sickness during the first two years of his probation.

208. The Station applying for aid from this Fund must show the amount of hired help that has been employed on the Station; and if such help has not been obtained, must show how the appointments have been supplied.

209. The Stations which may have claims on the Fund shall pay the sick preachers their allowances, and the Stations shall apply, according to rule, for their claims on the Fund.

210. The time allowed for a probationer being on the Fund shall not be longer than six months; and that of a preacher in full connexion shall not be more than 15 months.

Conference Fund.

211. This Fund is raised in the same way as the preceeding; at the same time; the same amount; and disposed of in the same way, being *finally* carried to the General Treasurer's account.

212. It is appropriated in paying Incidental Charges; and the Travelling Allowances of Delegates to Conference, including the General Officers; and General Committee Delegates expenses to District Meetings.

Children's Fund.

213. This Fund is raised by the Circuits and Missions, and the amounts paid, through the General Secretary, to the Connexional Treasurer; and is under the control and direction of the Conference.

214. A *Select* Committee is appointed by *each* Conference, to apportion the sum each Station must pay quarterly to this Fund; their Report to be sanctioned by Conference, and published in the Conference Minutes.

215. Each Married Minister shall receive for each of his Children, born in the Ministry, up to sixteen years of age, $6.50 per quarter; but no allowance is made to a Minister's Children born during his Probation.

216. On the event of a Minister's demise, leaving Children, the aforesaid allowances shall be continued to such Children until sixteen years of age.

Beneficent Fund.

217. This fund is supported by grants, subscriptions, donations and bequests. The Quarterly Meetings and individuals are earnestly requested to subscribe liberally to sustain it, seeing that our Superannuated Ministers in Canada are dependent upon it. It has been hitherto assisted from the English Book-room establishment, but other sources of aid are much required.

218. Each minister is requested to raise for this fund at least $2.50 per year.

219. Every travelling preacher who has been superanuated by the Conference shall receive an allowance from this Fund, according to the following Table. The years of travelling are reckoned from one Conference to another; and the allowance is made for uninterrupted Service.

a. If any minister shall marry a woman fifteen years younger than himself, and afterwards leave her a widow, she shall receive no benefit from this fund.

b. Any Minister marrying while he is superannuated, and afterwards leaving his wife a widow, she shall receive no allowance from this fund unless he resume the itinerant work.

Years.	Allowances.	Years.	Allowances.	Years.	Allowance.
	$ c.		$ c.		$ c.
8	19 46	19	59 64	30	99 76
9	23 11	20	63 26	31	103 41
10	26 76	21	66 91	32	107 06
11	30 41	22	70 56	33	111 93
12	34 06	23	74 21	34	116 80
13	37 71	24	77 86	35	121 66
14	41 36	25	81 51	36	126 53
15	45 01	26	85 16	37	131 40
16	48 66	27	88 81	38	136 26
17	52 31	28	92 46	39	141 13
18	55 96	29	96 11	40	146 00

220. Annuities to Minister's widows are allowed according to the following Scale, which is regulated by the number of years their husbands have travelled.

Years.	Allowance.	Years.	Allowance.	Years.	Allowance.
	$ c.		$ c.		$ c.
10	9 73	21	36 40	32	68 13
11	12 16	22	38 93	33	73 00
12	14 60	23	41 36	34	77 68
13	17 03	24	43 80	35	82 73
14	19 46	25	46 23	36	87 60
15	21 89	26	48 66	37	92 46
16	24 33	27	51 09	38	97 33
17	26 76	28	53 53	39	102 20
18	29 20	29	55 96	40	107 06
19	31 63	30	58 40		
20	34 06	31	63 26		

221. An allowance of two shillings stirling per week shall be granted to each child of a deceased Minister, when the mother is also dead, until it attains the age of eighteen years, provided due application be made by the superintendent of the station in which such orphan resides. The remittance shall be made through the superintendent preacher.

Beneficent Fund Collection.

222. One Collection shall be taken up each year, in the month of November, at every appointment in Canada, in behalf of this Fund, and the amount so collected shall be certified on the Annual Report to District Meeting.

Examination of Probationary Ministers and Candidates for the Ministry—Central Board.

223. A Central Examining Committee shall be appointed by the Conference, consisting of six Ministers, one of whom shall be the Secretary of the Board, who shall send to the District Secretaries a sufficient number of examination papers for all the Probationary ministers in the work, not later than two weeks previous to each examination. He shall also conduct the correspondence of the Board, and be the Convener thereof.

224. This Committee shall prepare the questions on the books of study for the Probationary Ministers and Candidates for the Ministry. They shall also examine the written answers to questions sent to them by the Secretaries of District Boards, and report to the District Meetings and Conference the result of their examination.

225. The Committee shall meet on the Tuesday previous to the fourth meeting of the General Committee, to prepare the Report, and at such other times during each year as may be necessary for the proper discharge of its duties.

226. The necessary expenses of this Committee shall be paid from the Ministerial Examiners' Fund, which shall be sustained by the stations taking up collections in the month of May for it annually, in the proportion of one collection to each Minister laboring on a Station.

District Boards.

227. A Committee shall be appointed by Conference for each District, consisting of three or four Ministers, of whom one shall be the Secretary, who shall take charge of the printed questions sent to him by the Secretary of the Central Board; lay them before the Probationers, or Candidates, at the time of Examination; and when the time marked on them has expired, again take charge of them and the written answers, both of which he shall send to the Examiner of the Central Board whose name the printed paper bears.

228. They shall meet, 1st., on the first Tuesday in September, to conduct the examination on that part of the course of study which the Central Board has directed to be taken up for the first half of the year; 2nd., on the first Tuesday in April, to conduct the examination on the remainder of the studies; also to examine Candidates for the Ministry who have been recommended by the February Quarterly Meetings; and 3rd., the day previous to District Meeting to examine and report upon the Journals of Probationers.

229. At the September Meeting, they shall examine Probationers verbally on the Discipline of the Church; on cases

of Discipline; on the management of Church Affairs, Revival Efforts, Pastoral Duties, and other matters of a kindred practical character. They shall send a report of said Examination for the Central Board of Examiners.

If a District is geographically too large for all to meet conveniently in one place, the Central Committee may divide it into two sections, and appoint another Secretary.

Candidates for the Ministry.

230. Each Candidate, recommended according to rule, shall, before being called to enter upon the work of the Ministry, undergo an examination before the Board of Examiners for his District, upon the following subjects:—

- (a.) On the Canonical Books of the Old and New Testaments, in the present authorized version.
- (b.) On the Fundamental Doctrines of these Testaments, as stated in the Discipline of the Church, and as explained by Wesley, Cooke, Garner and other Methodist writers.
- (c.) On Grammar, Geography, Arithmetic, Reading and writing. The Candidate to read a chapter of the Bible, and write from dictation any passage that may be given him.
- (d.) On his call to the Ministry; on Pastoral Work; and on Sermonizing. The Candidate to produce a written Sermon, for the satisfaction of the Board.

231. The Board shall report said Examination, with recommendation, or non-recommendation, of the Candidate to the ensuing District Meeting, General Committee, or General Missionary Committee, as the case may require.

Probationer's Course of Study shall be:—

223. *1st Year*—Analytical and Practical Grammar; Colliers British History; Petty's Connexional History;* Petty's Tract on the Polity of the Primitive Methodist Church;* Angus' Handbook to the Bible;† and Garner's Theology.*

2nd Year.—Analytical and Practical Grammar; Murray's Logic; Wayland's Moral Science;† Cooke's Theology;* and Wesley's Sermons.

3rd Year.—White's Universal History; Whately's Rhetoric;‡ Kidder's Homiletics; Kirk's Bible and Modern Thought; and Watson's Institutes, vols. 1 and 2.

4th Year.—White's Eighteen Centuries; Upham's Mental Science;§ Horne's Introduction; Watson's Institutes, vols. 3 and 4; and Ulster Prize Essays, or Gold and the Gospel.**

The following Works are recommended for consultation, which it is hoped will be secured and studied:—

1st Year.—Quakenbos' Composition; Todd's Manual; Clarke's Letter; Clowes' Life; and Bastow's Dictionary.

2nd Year.—Angus' Hand-book to the English tongue; Paley's Evidences; James' Earnest Ministry; and Crompton's agency of the Church.

3rd Year.—Angus' Hand-Book of English Literature; Pinnock's Catechism of Church History; Dunn's Science and Christian Thought; and Stephen's Methodism.

4th Year.—Paley's Horæ Paulinæ; Birk's Exodus; Hibbert or Mill, on Baptism.; Pearson on the Creed; and Locke on the Understanding.

* Primitive Methodist Book-Room. † London Tract Society's Edition. ‡ Harper's New York Edition. § Ward & Co., London. ** Nisbit's Edition.

MISCELLANEOUS REGULATIONS.

MINISTERS.

Resignation of Ministers.

233. That in the event of any Minister tendering his resignation during the Conference year no credential shall be given him till the following Conference.

Family Visiting.

234. Each minister is expected to make fifteen pastoral visits weekly, on an average, during the year. If such a number of visits be not performed, the reasons why such is the case must be sent to the Conference; and it shall decide whether they are satisfactory.

Beneficence Sermon.

235. Each preacher shall preach once a year on Scriptural beneficence.

Conveyance of Church Property.

236. Previously to building churches and parsonages, the Superintendent preacher of the Station shall see that Conveyance deeds of such property be properly made.

Ministerial Widowers.

237. The time of a Minister receiving his usual salary, in case of his becoming a widower, shall not be less than one year after becoming such.

Ministers Removing.

238. Ministers removing shall leave their stations the last Monday but one in June, and shall be on their new stations on or before the first Saturday in July.

Editor, Book Steward, and Missionary Secretary.

239. Brethren appointed Editor, Book Steward, and Missionary Secretary, shall continue in said offices no longer than five years consecutively; and they shall be liable to removal by any Conference during that time; and their removal shall be *absolute* at the expiration of five Connectional years.

PROBATION MINISTERS.

First Year of Travelling.

240. When a young man has travelled ten months, and all is satisfactory relative to him in the Ministry, such period of time shall be reckoned the first year of his probation.

Probationers Marrying.

141. If a minister marry during his probation he shall be discontinued as a regular Travelling Preacher.

Probationer's Journal.

242. Probationers shall be required to keep a journal for three months during each year of the first three years of their probation, and the whole of the fourth year; and such Journal shall be submitted each year to the Board of Examiners.

Probationers Smoking.

243. In future no preacher on probation shall be received into full connexion and ordained, unless it be stated on his Station's report that he has not used tobacco during the previous year.—(1868, Page 9.)

Probationers and University Studies.

224. A young man attending and graduating at the University with a view to our Ministry, and who has laboured on the Toronto Circuit under the supervision of its ministers shall have allowed one year's probation for each two year's study.

Superannuated Ministers.

225. When a Minister is duly Superannuated, his travelling expenses shall be paid him from the Station on which he is superannuated to the place where he may choose to reside, provided that each place is within the province of Ontario.

Superannuated Ministers in Conference.

246. All Superannuated Ministers of twenty years standing shall be allowed a seat and voice in Conference.

OTHER MISCELLANEOUS REGULATIONS.

Mission Circuits and Removals.

247. Stations on becoming Mission Circuits without their consultation shall have the removal expenses of their ministers to them, for the first year, paid out of the Mission Fund.

Conference Delegation at District Meetings.

248. The District Meetings shall as far as convenient appoint brethren to represent them in Conference who are in attendance at the District Meetings ; but this should not be acted out in all cases, inasmuch as some brethren, very suitable to be Conference Delegates, might not attend District Meeting.

Hired Local Preacher Delegates to Conference.

249. Any one who has laboured continuously as a hired local preacher for seven years shall be eligible for election from District Meeting to Conference, as a Ministerial Delegate.

Deficiencies of Salaries.

250. When deficiencies exist on Missions, appeals to Conference shall be allowed ; and if the state of the Mission Fund permits, such deficiencies shall be paid in part, so that

each married Missionary shall not be more than $50.00 deficient for any given year, and no unmarried Missionary any more than $25.00, unless the Conference is assured that such Missionaries have neglected their duties.

Extraordinary Income.

251. All money raised on Missions for Ministers use from re-unions, Socials, Tea-parties, or any other source, shall be reported on the Yearly Report of the Mission as forming part of the income of the Station.

Finance Committee.

252. The members of the Granting Committee, as appointed by the District Meetings, shall compose this Committee, and the Missionary Secretary, by virtue of office, shall be a member of it.

Quarterly Income.

253. Every station is earnestly requested to adopt the Schedule system, as contained in the Schedules prepared by the Book Room, in order to increase the Quarterly Income.

Church Property Reported.

254. The question on our Annual Report Form :—"What is the value of our Church Property?" shall be followed by this one :—What is the amount of debt on the said property?

Church Building on Missions.

255. No Mission Station shall Commence building a new church until the District Committee has given its sanction.

Children's Fund and Mission Circuits.

256. Missions becoming Mission Circuits shall pay to the Children's Fund the first year one-third of the apportionment, the second year one-half, the third year two-thirds, the fourth year three-fourths, after which the whole of the amount shall be paid.

Prizes to Juvenile Collectors.

257. Stations are allowed to give one per cent. in books to Juvenile Collectors for our Missionary Society, when the authorities believe such distribution of prizes will encourage the Collectors.

Reading the Rules.

258. Ministers who have travelled under ten years are *required* to read the Discipline and the rules made by each succeeding Conference *once in every six months*, and state whether they have done so, in the Station Reports to District Meeting and Conference.

259. All our Ministers and lay officials are earnestly requested to acquaint themselves well with the rules of the Church, that they may be prepared to take a just and constitutional course at all business Meetings.

Ministers' Salary.

260. To a single minister in full connexion $200. To a married minister on Probation $320. To a single minister on Probation $160 a year.

N.B. The last clause was omitted in its proper place, and not discovered until the type was distributed.

Church Services.

BAPTISM.

BAPTISM OF INFANTS.

When Baptism is administered to Infants, the Minister may give an extemporary address, or use the following:

And they brought young children to him, that he should touch them, and his disciples rebuked those that brought them.

But when Jesus saw it, he was much displeased, and said, Suffer little children to come unto me, and forbid them not, for of such is the kingdom of God.

And he took them in his arms, and put his hands upon them, and blessed them.

Mark x. 13, &c.

At the same time came the disciples unto Jesus, saying, Who is the greatest in the kingdom of heaven? and Jesus called a little child unto him, and set him in the midst of them.

And said, Verily I say unto you, except ye be converted, and become as little children, ye shall not enter into the kingdom of heaven.

Whosoever therefore shall humble himself as this little child, the same is greatest in the kingdom of heaven.

And whoso shall receive one such little child in my name, receiveth me.

Matt. xviii. 1, &c.

From these Holy Scriptures, it is plain that the example and words of Jesus teach the duty of bringing our children to him; and also, that the Church should manifest care and solicitude in their behalf. The innocence of children is a likeness of that guileless simplicity which true religion stamps upon its possessor.

When children die in infancy, or before they know the difference between good and evil, we believe they are admitted into heaven; and if so, should they not be brought to the Saviour now, in the ordinance of baptism; and as far as circumstances will allow, be suitably recognized by the Church upon earth?

Baptism is an ordinance in which water is applied in the name of the *Holy Trinity*. "Go ye therefore," said Jesus, "and teach all nations, baptizing them in the name of the Father, and of the Son, and of the Holy Ghost."

If it be asked, what are the uses of baptism? the answer is,—1st. Every instance in which the ordinance is performed, in the scriptural use of sound words, it proclaims the nature of the Godhead, as consisting of Father, Son, and Holy Ghost; 2nd, it is a visible sign of human depravity, and of the regenerating influence of the Holy Spirit; for, an ordinance enjoining the application of water implies that we are unclean; and as water is an emblem of the Holy Spirit its use in baptism symbolizes the shedding forth of the Spirit's influence to purify our hearts; and 3rdly, baptism confers a blessing even on the infant subject. It is a solemn dedication of the child to God; it secures the prayers of parents, minister, and congregation; and it is a formal recognition of the child by the Church.

TO PARENTS.

You have great responsibilities in respect of this child: it is a young immortal; and therefore will never cease to be. Your influence, example, and teaching will make imperishable impressions upon your child's mind, if spared to you: let those impressions be against evil, and in favour of what is good. Should the child live, teach him the evil of the human heart; the need of Jesus Christ as a Saviour; and that there is salvation through the atonement of his cross; and make it your highest endeavour to lead your child to God, through Jesus Christ, that after leading a godly life on earth there may be the attainment of everlasting life in heaven.

The Minister naming the child, shall sprinkle or pour water upon it, saying,

I Baptize thee in the name of the Father, and of the Son, and of the Holy Ghost.

The Minister can then close with extemporary prayer, or use the following form of prayer.

LET US PRAY!

Almighty and everlasting God, we give thee hearty thanks for the abundant grace provided in the gospel covenant both for us and our children. May the baptism of the Holy Ghost come upon us that we may be purged from all moral defilement and renewed in righteousness and true holiness. We beseech thee to bless this child, and may he (or she) receive the inward and spiritual grace of which baptism is the sign, and should life be spared, may he be a seed to serve thee. We pray also that thou wouldst bless the parents of this child, whom we trust, with earnest sincerity, have offered to thee in baptism, the child thou hast given them. Help them to train him up in thy nurture and admonition in the way he should go, that in the maturity of future life he may not depart from it. Be gracious to us O Father, and to our children evermore, through Jesus Christ our Lord, Amen.

May the grace of of our Lord Jesus Christ, the Love of God the Father; the fellowship of the Holy Spirit be with us now and for evermore, Amen.

ADULT BAPTISM.

———:o:———

In administering Baptism to Adults, the Minister may use the following words of Holy Scripture:

There was a man of the Pharasees named Nicodemus, a ruler of the Jews.

The same came to Jesus by night, and said unto him, Rabbi, we know that thou art a teacher come from God, for no man can do these miracles that thou doest except God be with him.

Jesus answered, and said unto him, Verily, verily, I say unto thee, except a man be born again, he cannot see the kingdom of God.

Nicodemus saith unto him, How can a man be born when he is old? can he enter the second time into his mother's womb and be born?

Jesus answered, Verily, verily, I say unto thee except a man be born of water and of the Spirit he cannot enter into the kingdom of God.

That which is born of the flesh is flesh, and that which is born of the Spirit is spirit.

Marvel not that I said unto thee, Ye must be born again.

John iii. 1, &c.

Baptism is not regeneration: no mere ceremony can regenerate the heart; that great change is effected only by the Holy Spirit. Simon the sorcerer was baptized, yet remained unchanged, for Peter said of him, "I perceive thou art in the gall of bitterness and in the bond of iniquity."—Acts viii. 23. "He is not a Jew who is one outwardly, neither is that circumcision which is outward in the flesh; but he is a Jew which is one inwardly, and circumcision is that of the heart, in the spirit and not in the letter, whose praise is not of men but of God." Rest not, then, without regenerating grace, of which baptism is the sign.

This ordinance confers a benefit on the adult subject of baptism, as by it he is admitted into the visible Church of God, and enters upon its privileges, with the prayers of God's people, in connection with his solemn profession of the Christian faith.

The Minister shall say to the person to be baptized:

Dost thou believe in God the Father who created all things, and in Jesus Christ his Son, who is equal with the Father, who came into the world to save sinners, who died for our sins and rose again for our justification, and who is now at the right hand of God, our exalted Prince and Saviour, and who will one day judge the world in righteousness? Dost thou believe in the Holy Ghost, the third person in the Godhead, whose office it is to enlighten and purify our hearts, and apply the blessings of salvation to those who believe the gospel? Dost thou believe in the forgiveness of sins, in the resurrection of the body, and in life everlasting, through Jesus Christ? And dost thou believe in the future condemnation and punishment of the wicked?

The person to be baptized shall say :

I believe this.

And the Minister shall then ask :

Wilt thou endeavour to love the Lord thy God; obediently keep his holy will and commandments; living a life of faith on Jesus Christ thy Saviour?

The person to be baptized shall answer :

I will endeavour to do so, God helping me.

The Minister then naming him, shall say :

I baptize thee in the name of the Father, and of the Son and of the Holy Ghost.

Close with prayer and the usual benediction.

MATRIMONY.

―――:o:―――

SOLEMNIZATION OF MATRIMONY.

The Banns of those to be married must be published in the Congregation three several Sundays, in the time of Divine Service, unless they be otherwise qualified according to law.

FORM OF BANNS.

I publish the Banns of Marriage between J. B., of ―――, and M. C., of ―――; if any of you know cause or just impediment why these two persons should not be joined together in holy matrimony, ye are to declare it. This is the first (second or third) time of asking.

MARRIAGE FORM.

When marriage is solemnized, the persons to be married standing together, the man on the right hand and the woman on the left, the Minister may address them in the following words :

We are met in the sight of God, and in the presence of these witnesses, to join together this man and woman in holy matrimony, which is an honourable estate instituted by

God in the time of man's innocency, when he made the woman, formed the union between the man and her, and said, "They shall be one flesh." The Saviour also affirmed the nuptial covenant to be a bond instituted of God, when he said, "What God hath joined together, let no man put asunder." Hence, matrimony is not only lawful, but in perfect accordance with the will of God, and of Divine appointment.

Were it only a mere civil contract, an alliance of convenience and interest, in which heart and principle have little share, it would not be such a solemn and momentous engagement; but considering its nature and solemnity, it ought to be entered upon carefully, sincerely, and in the fear of the Lord.

The Minister shall then say:

I require you both, as ye will have to answer at the awful day of judgment, if either of you know any impediment why you may not be joined together in holy matrimony, you now confess it, for be assured, that so many as are married otherwise than God's law allows, are not joined together by God, neither is their matrimony lawful.

If no impediment be known, the Minister shall say to the man:

Wilt thou have this woman to be thy lawful wedded wife? wilt thou love, comfort, and cherish her? and keep her in sickness and in health, to live together after God's ordinance?

The man shall answer:

I will.

To the woman:

Wilt thou have this man to be thy lawful wedded husband? wilt thou love, honour and obey him, and keep him in sickness and in health, to live together after God's ordinance.

The woman shall answer:

I will.

The Minister shall cause the man with his right hand to take the woman by her right hand, and say after him:

I, J. B., take thee M. C., to be my lawful wedded wife, from this day forward, for better for worse, in prosperity or adversity, in sickness and in health, till parted by death.

Then the woman, with her right hand taking the man by his right hand, shall say after the Minister:

I, M. C., take thee, J. B., to be my lawful wedded husband, from this day forward, for better for worse, in prosperity or adversity, in sickness and in health, till parted by death.

If a ring be used, the man should put it on the fourth finger of the woman's left hand, according to custom.

And the Minister shall say:

Inasmuch as these persons, J. B. and M. C., have declared

their mutual consent to enter into matrimony, and engaged to live therein according to God's ordinance, let all present witness that they are man and wife, agreeably to the word of God and the law of this land. Those whom God hath joined together, let no man put asunder.

ADDRESS.

To the Husband:

HUSBANDS love your wives, even as Christ also loved the church, and gave himself for it:

He that loveth his wife, loveth himself.

For no man ever yet hated his own flesh, but nourisheth and cherisheth it, even as the Lord the church.

For we are members of his body, of his flesh, and of his bones.

For this cause shall a man leave his father and his mother, and be joined unto his wife, and they two shall be one flesh.

Eph. v. 25, &c.

To the wife:

WIVES submit yourselves unto your own husbands, as unto the Lord.

For the husband is the head of the wife, even as Christ is the head of the Church; and he is the Saviour of the body.

Therefore *as* the church is subject unto Christ, so let the wives to be to their own husbands in everything.

Eph. v. 2, &c.

To them both:

Nevertheless, let every one in particular so love his wife even as himself; and the wife see that she reverence her husband.

Eph. v. 33.

It is proposed that the Minister close with an extemporary prayer; but if he prefer the following form of words, he can use them:

Almighty and everlasting Father, who art the creator and preserver of men, and the God of all goodness, visit us now with thy blessing: deal not with us according to our sins, nor reward us according to our iniquities, but may Thy mercy save us, and thy power defend us. Especially, O God, be gracious to this man and woman, who have been united in the closest of earthly relationships. May peace and love dwell within their borders. Direct them, in Thy wisdom, through the changing scenes of life. Confer upon them the gifts and graces of thy Holy Spirit, that they may sincerely love and humbly serve Thee; and walking in Thy commandments and ordinances blamelessly, they may command their household after them; and by Thy rich grace, may they attain at last eternal life. We ask these and every blessing through Jesus Christ our Lord. Amen.

Close with the benediction.

THE LORD'S SUPPER.

First, let a suitable Hymn be sung, and prayer offered.

SACRAMENT PRAYER.

* O Lord our Father in Jesus Christ we now present ourselves before thee with gratitude and confidence,—with gratitude for the gift and atoning work of thy dear Son, and with confidence in the sufficiency of his sacrifice offered for our sins. O God we would humbly confess our sinfulness and guilt, and acknowledge our dessert of thy wrath. We confess also to our entire helplessness to deliver ourselves from the awful curse to which our sins have exposed us. There is no help in us. But we turn to Jesus who died on the cross for us. Herein is love, not that we loved God, but that thou lovedst us, and didst send thy Son to be the propitiation for our sins. We come to thee in consideration of the fact that He suffered for sin, the just for the unjust to bring us to God. We now are invited into communion with thee in celebrating that wonderful love by which our redemption has been procured. We thank thee for this blessed ordinance. It is a light and guide into thy presence. It is a standing memorial of infinite love coming to meet our souls needs. O that the great things represented here may deeply impress our hearts, and may we be participants in the saving benefits thereof. Sprinkle our hearts now with the blood of the new covenant, that we may be cleansed from all unrighteousness and be assured of thy favour. Also, O God, make us increase and abound in love to thee, to one another, and toward all men. Raise our affections evermore to things above, and while we show our Lord's death, may we joyfully anticipate his glorious appearing at the last day. Here our prayers, O Lord, and fulfil in us the good pleasure of thy will for the sake of Jesus Christ our strength and Redeemer. Amen.

Then let the Minister read the following Scriptures, or give an extemporary address, or do both, in part, as he feels disposed, under the circumstances.

And as they were eating, Jesus took bread and blessed it, and brake it, and gave it to the disciples, and said, Take, eat; this is my body which is given for you: this do in remembrance of me.

Matt. xxvi. 26. Luke xxii. 19.

And he took the cup, and gave thanks, and gave it to them, saying, Drink ye all of it; for this is my blood of the new testament, which is shed for many, for the remission of sins: this cup is the new testament in my blood, which is shed for you.

Matt. xxvi. 27, 28. Luke xxii. 20.

Also read the Apostle Paul's words to the Corinthians.

For I have received of the Lord that which also I delivered unto you, that the Lord Jesus the same night in which he was betrayed took bread:

And when he had given thanks, he brake it, and said, Take, eat; this is my body which is broken for you, do this in remembrance of me.

After the same manner also he took the cup, when he had supped, saying, This cup is the new testament in my blood; this do ye, as oft as ye drink it, in remembrance of me.

For as often as ye eat this bread and drink this cup, ye do show the Lord's death till he come.

Wherefore, whosoever shall eat this bread and drink this cup of the Lord unworthily, shall be guilty of the body and blood of the Lord.

But let a man examine himself, and so let him eat of that bread and drink of that cup.

For he that eateth and drinketh unworthily, eateth and drinketh damnation (judgment or condemnation) to himself, not discerning the Lord's body.

1 Cor. xi. 23, &c.

Beloved friends, those who eat and drink unworthily at the table of the Lord, are such as venture to come, and have not the fervent sincerity and devotion which God requires; nor a true purpose of heart to be the deciples of Jesus Christ. This is to commune at the table of the Lord unworthily; and whosoever does so is condemned: condemned by his conscience, and condemned before God; for "whatsoever is not of faith is sin."

But though as Christians we be deeply sensible of our general unworthiness, yet, if we now have faith in Christ, if we now are his deciples, if we now indeed love the Lord, and are walking before him in his fear, we may come to his table and welcome; yea, we should esteem it our bounden duty to come, and commemorate the Saviour's dying love. Come then, gather round his cross, and in view of Calvary's hallowed scenes, renew again your plighted vows and faith to our dying Lord.

And you penitent sinners, (if such there be,) even you, while turning to the Lord with true repentance and sincerity of heart, may come also, and seek the Saviour at his table. Yes, you may come with your burden of sin, your broken hearts, your harrassings of guilt, and your unutterable wretchedness: here you may cast yourselves by humble faith upon him who died for you.

Come one and all, who are true believers or true penitents: come, take the emblems of the Saviour's love; and prove by faith that his flesh is meat indeed, and his blood drink indeed, to your souls.

Then let the Minister first receive the Communion in both kinds himself.

And as the bread and cup are given into the hands of the people, let him use the Saviour's words, interspersing other suitable expressions that may occur to his mind.

THE BREAD.

Jesus said, "Take, eat; this is my body which is given for you: this do in remembrance of me." Feed by faith on Christ, who is the bread of life.

THE CUP.

The Saviour said, "This cup is the new testament in my blood, which is shed for you." Trust by faith in the blood of Christ for purity of heart, and meetness for heaven.

Close with prayer and the benediction.

BURIAL OF THE DEAD.

The Minister on meeting the corpse, may read:

I am the resurrection and the life, saith the Lord : he that believeth in me, though he were dead, yet shall he live ; and whosoever liveth and believeth in me, shall never die.

John xi. 25, &c.

We brought nothing into this world, and it is certain we can carry nothing out. The Lord gave, and the Lord hath taken away ; blessed be the name of the Lord.

Tim. vi. 7.   Job i. 21.

I know that my redeemer liveth, and that he shall stand at the latter day upon the earth. And though after my skin worms destroy this body, yet in my flesh shall I see God ; whom I shall see for myself, and mine eyes shall behold, and not another.

Job. xiv. 25, &c.

Man that is born of a woman is of few days, and full of trouble.

He cometh forth like a flower, and is cut down ; he fleeth also as a shadow, and continueth not.

Job. xix. 1, 2.

Man dieth and wasteth away; yea, man giveth up the ghost, and where is he.

Job. xiv. 10.

When the corpse is laid in the earth.

My days are past; my purposes are broken off: even the thoughts of my heart.

If I wait, the grave is mine house; I have made my bed in darkness.

I have said to corruption, thou art my father; and to the worm, thou art my mother and my sister.

Job xvii. 11, 14.

Forasmuch as it hath pleased Almighty God to take away the soul of our brother (or sister) departed, we therefore commit his body to the ground; earth to earth, ashes to ashes, dust to dust, in hope of the resurrection to eternal life through our Lord Jesus Christ, who shall change our vile body that it may be like unto his glorious body according to the mighty working whereby he is able to subdue all things unto himself.

On the Resurrection:

But now is Christ risen from the dead, and become the first fruits of them that slept.

1 Cor. xv. 20.

Now this I say brethren, that flesh and blood cannot inherit the kingdom of God, neither doth corruption inherit incorruption.

Behold, I show you a mystery: we shall not all sleep, but we shall all be changed.

In a moment, in the twinkling of an eye, at the last trump: for the trumpet shall sound, and the dead shall be raised incorruptible, and we shall be changed.

For this corruptible shall put on incorruption, and this mortal shall put on immortality.

So when this corruptible shall have put on incorruption, and this mortal shall have put on immortality, then shall be brought to pass the saying that is written, Death is swallowed up in victory.

O death, where is thy sting: O grave, where is thy victory?

The sting of death is sin, and the strength of sin is the law:

But thanks be to God who giveth us the victory through our Lord Jesus Christ.

Therefore my beloved brethren be ye steadfast, unmovable, always abounding in the work of the Lord, forasmuch as ye know that your labour is not in vain in the Lord.

1 Cor. 14, 50, &c.

Beloved friends, let us all remember, that as it is now with the departed, whose body we are committing to the grave, so it will shortly be with us.

Death is unspeakably solemn: it is the doorway that leads into eternity; and we certainly must all soon pass through it, to our final destination. Behold we go the way of all the earth. He who is then filthy, will be filthy still; and he who is holy, will be holy still.

That death may be without sting to us: that the grave may be stript of its terrors; and that we may have, while in this mortal state, glorious hopes of a joyful resurrection to everlasting life, let us seek by faith a personal interest in the precious blood of Jesus Christ our Lord. This only can fit us for living, prepare us for dying, and qualify our souls for heaven." I heard a voice from heaven saying unto me, write, blessed are the dead which die in the Lord from henceforth :—Yea saith the *Spirit* that they may rest from their labours, and their works do follow them.

The Minister may then close with prayer and the benediction.

LET US PRAY :

Almighty God in whom we live and have being, in whose hands our breath is and whose are all our ways, we beseech thee to give us the spirit of wisdom, of grace, and of thy fear. Pardon all our sins for thy name and mercy's sake, and for the sake of Jesus Christ who died for us; Help us also to walk before thee in the land of the living. Assist us, O Lord, constantly to remember the solemn facts of our frailty and the certainty of our speedy departure from this world. Deeply impress on our minds, a sense of the great responsibilities and duties that devolve upon us while on earth, that we may so number our days as to apply our hearts unto wisdom. O heavenly Father, enlighten our minds by thy Holy Spirit, and dispose our hearts that we may know thy saving truth and be doers of the work thou hast allotted us in the present life. Raise us from the death of sin to the life of righteousness. Help us to serve thee all our days, that when death comes to us, we may depart in peace, and at the general resurrection be found acceptable in thy sight. And O, may the blessing pronounced by our gracious Saviour be then our portion. "Come ye blessed of my Father, inherit the kingdom prepared for you from the foundation of the world.

The grace of our Lord Jesus Christ, the love of God, and the fellowship of the Holy Ghost be with us all, now and forever. Amen.

FORM OF
THE
DEDICATION OF A CHURCH.

—:o:—

Beloved Friends.—It is meet and right that houses should be erected for the public worship of God, and set apart for religious uses. The scriptures teach that God is well pleased with those who build temples to the honour of his name, and in order to meet the religious wants of men. By the command of God, Moses built the Tabernacle, and called upon the people to bring their offerings of gold and silver and precious stones, and other materials for the performance of the work. And when it had been set up, the glory of the Lord filled the Tabernacle. In obedience to appointment and directions from God, Solomon built the Temple, and when dedicated, it was under signal proofs of His approbation; for he also filled the temple with His glory. Let us believe that He will approve our work in erecting and dedicating this house for religious worship; let us also join in praise to Almighty God, that this godly undertaking has been so far completed, and in prayer for this further blessing upon all who shall hereafter worship in this place.

Let an appropriate hymn be sung and extemporate prayer offered, the congregation kneeling.

Then let the following Lessons be read:—

First Lesson. 2 Chron. 6, 1, 2, 18-21., 41, 42., vii. 1-4. Then said Solomon, the Lord hath said that He would dwell in the darkness. But I have built a house of habitation for thee, and a place for thy dwelling forever.

But will God in very deed dwell with men on the earth ? Behold heaven and the heaven of heavens cannot contain thee, how much less this house that I have built! Have respect therefore unto the prayer of thy servant, and to his supplication, O Lord my God, to hearken unto the cry and the prayer which thy servant prayeth before thee; that thine eyes may be open upon this house day and night, upon the place whereof thou hast said thou would'st put thy name there ; to hearken unto the prayer which thy servant prayeth toward this place. Hearken therefore unto the supplication of thy servant, and of thy people Israel, which they shall make toward this place, hear them from thy dwelling-place, even from heaven ; and when thou hearest forgive.

Now, therefore, arise O Lord God into thy resting place, thou and the ark of thy strength : let thy priests, O Lord God, be clothed with salvation, and let thy saints rejoice in goodness.

Now when Solomon had made an end of praying, the fire came down from heaven and consumed the burnt offering and the sacrifices ; and the glory of the Lord had filled the house. And the priests could not enter into the house of the Lord, because the glory of the Lord had filled the Lord's house. And when all the children of Israel saw how the fire came down and the glory of the Lord upon the house, they bowed themselves with their faces to the ground upon the pavement, and worshiped, and praised the Lord, saying for He is good; for his mercy endureth for ever. Then the king and all the people offered sacrifices before the Lord.

The Second Lesson. Ps. 122.

I was glad when they said unto me let us go into the house of the Lord. Our feet shall stand within thy gates O Jerusalem. Jerusalem is builded as a city that is compact together. Whither the tribes go up, the tribes of the Lord, unto the testimony of Israel to give thanks unto the name of the Lord. For there are set thrones of judgment, the thrones of the house of David. Pray for the peace of Jerusalem : they shall prosper that love thee. Peace be within thy walls, and prosperity within thy palaces. For my brethren and companion's sakes I will now say peace be within thee. Because of the house of the Lord our God I will seek thy good.

Third Lesson. Heb. 10. 19.

Having therefore brethren boldness to enter into the holiest by the blood of Jesus, by a new and living way which he hath consecrated for us through the veil that is to say his flesh ; and having a High Priest over the house of God ; let us draw near with a true heart in full assurance of faith, having our hearts sprinkled from an evil conscience, and our bodies washed with pure water. Let us hold fast the profession of our faith without wavering; (for he is faithful that promised) and let us consider one another to provoke unto love and good works ; not forsaking the assembling of ourselves, as the manner of some is; but exhorting one another; and so much the more as ye see the day approaching.

Then shall a hymn be sung, and a sermon delivered, and after Sermon the contributions of the people shall be received.

Then the Minister shall request the Congregation to stand while he repeats the following

DECLARATION.

Beloved Friends.—We are now assembled for the purpose of dedicating this house to the worship and service of God. With gratitude therefore to Him, who has so far blessed his servants in their undertaking to erect this church, we dedicate it for the reading of the word of God, the preaching of the gospel, the administration of the Christian Sacraments, and for public religious worship and Service according to the usages of the Primitive Methodist Church. Let us also at the same time solemnly dedicate ourselves anew to God as His true worshippers and servants. To Him let our bodies be dedicated that they may be fit temples for the indwelling of the Holy Ghost. To Him let our souls be dedicated that they may be renewed after the image of Christ. To Him let our lives be dedicated in the exercise of unceasing obedience. To Him let our labours and business be dedicated, that they may tend to the promotion of His glory, and the advancement of His kingdom in the earth.

The Congregation kneeling, the Minister shall offer the following prayer.

O Almighty God, we acknowledge that we are not worthy to offer any thing to thee; yet we beseech thee in thy great goodness to accept the dedication of this place to thy service. Hear the prayers and intercessions of all thy people who shall call upon thee in this House. May they approach thy sanctuary with humbleness and true devotion, and always perform a Service that is acceptable in thy sight, through Jesus Christ our Lord. Amen.

Grant, O Lord, that thy holy word read and preached in this place, may be grafted in the hearts of all who hear it, and may they thereby perceive and know what they ought to do in order to godliness of life and the salvation of their souls.

Bestow, O Lord, the influence of the Holy Ghost on thy servants whose duty it shall be to dispense the word of life here; and may the glorious gospel be proclaimed in its purity and simplicity and in the demonstration of the Holy Spirit, to the people assembling in this house, that many may thereby be brought to a knowledge of the truth as it is in Jesus Christ.

Arise O Lord and come unto this place. Let thine eye be open toward it day and night. Let thine ear be attent unto the prayers that shall be offered unto thee here. Hearken to them in heaven thy dwelling-place? and when thou hearest forgive. May we all, with thy people everywhere, grow up into a holy temple in the Lord, and at last have a place in thy Temple above. And to the Father, Son, and Holy Spirit, be everlasting praise.

The Service may conclude with the doxology and the benediction.

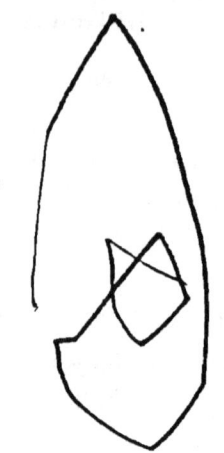

CONSTITUTION AND RULES

OF THE

Primitive Methodist Sunday Schools

IN CANADA.

"And these words, which I command thee this day, shall be in thine heart; and thou shalt teach them diligently unto thy children, and shalt talk of them when thou sittest in thine house, and when thou walkest by the way, and when thou liest down, and when thou risest up."—Deut. vi. 6, 7.

CONSTITUTION.

ARTICLE I.

This School shall be called "THE ——————— PRIMITIVE METHODIST SABBATH SCHOOL."

ARTICLE II.

The Officers shall be a Superintendent, Secretary, Treasurer, and Librarian, with assistants to these offices; all of whom shall be elected quarterly or annually.

ARTICLE III.

The Managers of the School shall be the above-named Officers, the Teachers, and the Minister in charge, who when present shall be chairman of all business meetings, by virtue of office.

ARTICLE IV.

Business Meetings of the School shall be held quarterly, just before the Quarter-day Board of the Station; and an Annual Meeting for the Election of Officers, etc., immediately after the Anniversary. A Special Business Meeting may be called by the Superintendent at any time, to meet cases of emergency.

ARTICLE V.

An Anniversary Service shall be held on the———— ————of each year, at which time a full report of the numerical and financial condition of the School shall be given to the public.

ARTICLE VI.

All the business transactions of the School shall, when desired, be submitted to the Quarterly Meeting of the Station; and no person shall continue to hold the office of Superintendent in any Connexional School without the sanction of this Board.

ARTICLE VII.

No person shall become, or continue an Officer or Teacher, whose character is immoral, or whose peculiar religious doctrines would be likely to promote discord in the School.

RULES.

TIME OF OPENING AND CLOSING.

The time for Opening and Closing this School shall be

OFFICERS' DUTIES.

2nd. MINISTERS. It shall be the duty of every Minister to regard the Sabbath School as an important part of his charge. He shall visit each School on his Station as often as convenient, in order that he may understand their wants and workings; also, to cultivate a style of address calculated to interest and benefit children, and by every possible means seek to promote their welfare.

SUPERINTENDENT.

3rd. It shall be the duty of the Superintendent to be in the School-Room at least five minutes before the time for opening School. He shall open and close the school with singing and prayer, or see that this is done by some other efficient person. He shall admit new Scholars, and see that their names are registered; promote to higher classes the deserving ones; provide substitutes for absent Teachers; announce the lesson for the day, and for the following Sabbath; give proper notice of business meetings to be held; and must dismiss the classes one by one. He shall enforce the rules for the maintenance of order in a kind, respectful, yet firm manner; and be himself a pattern in all good works.

SECRETARY.

It shall be the duty of the Secretary to keep a correct journal of all proceedings of Official Meetings; shall give notice to all absent persons affected by any resolution passed; shall call the Teachers' Roll at the opening of the School; shall renew the Class-Books; keep a record of all the Officers, Teachers, and Scholars, with the date of their entering and leaving School; keep an account of all moneys received and expended; prepare a Report for the Annual Meeting; and attend to any other duties, as directed by a Teachers' Meeting, or the Superintendent.

TREASURER.

It shall be the duty of the Treasurer to receive all moneys belonging to the School, and keep an account of the same; shall pay all accounts, when approved by the Teachers' Meeting; and shall at any time when requested give a statement of the state of the funds.

LIBRARIAN.

It shall be the duty of the Librarian to be present five minutes before the opening of the School, to supply all the Classes with Books, and see that the Books are properly collected and packed away. He shall keep a Catalogue of all Library Books, and distribute them to the Scholars, as directed by the Teachers' Meeting, taking care to report monthly to the Superintendent any books not returned to him at the proper time by Scholars or Teachers.

TEACHERS.

6th. It shall be the duty of all teachers to be at the head of their respective classes five minutes before the opening of school; to be regular in attendance; and should any teacher be absent without a sufficient reason for six weeks in succession, their membership as a teacher shall be forfeited.

They shall endeavour to instruct their scholars in the true meaning and intent of the holy scriptures; their duty to God, to their parents, guardians, teachers, to themselves, and to the world.

Shall enjoin upon them the keeping holy the Sabbath day; keeping good company; abstaining from the use of strong drink; and especially strive to lead their scholars to Christ—to trust, love, and obey Him—through whose merits alone they can find acceptance with God and eternal life.

CHILDREN.

7th. The children are expected to be present at the hour appointed, clean in their person and apparel; to submit to all the directions of their teachers; to learn the verses appointed out of the lesson for the day; and not to leave the school during school hours, without the consent of the teacher or superintendent. They shall also join in the singing exercises, and be orderly and reverent during prayer.

RECOMMENDATIONS.

1st. That a Teachers' Prayer Meeting be held in every Sabbath School at least once a Month.

2nd. That wherever practicable, a weekly meeting be held by the teachers, to study the lesson for the forthcoming Sabbath.

3rd. That our schools get their books, and other school requisites, at our Connexional Book Store, in Toronto.

4. That the foregoing Rules be read in every school, at least once a quarter.

These Sabbath School Rules can be had in separate form at the Book Room, at $1 per 100.

www.ingramcontent.com/pod-product-compliance
Lightning Source LLC
Chambersburg PA
CBHW031121160426
43192CB00008B/1069